SHAMELESS

SHAMELESS

How I lost my virginity and kept my faith

Dani Fankhauser

Second edition.

ISBN 978-0692965955

ReadThisNext Publishing

Book and cover design by Dani Fankhauser.

Dedicated to my parents.

Table of Contents

FIRSTS

One warm Friday afternoon my senior year of college, I came home to find the two-bedroom apartment I shared with three other girls empty. The four of us lived in a complex a few miles from our private Christian university, Point Loma Nazarene University in San Diego.

The balcony facing ours belonged to two guys, who we'd often see shirtless at their barbecue. One roommate suspected they were male strippers because they were fit, stayed home during the day, went out together in the evening, and didn't return until late at night. The boys were actually mixed martial artists training for the UFC.

I saw their apartment door ajar and could hear music loudly playing. With my roommates gone, I decided to walk over to introduce myself. It was completely out of character, as I was normally shy, but I was fulfilling a mission given to me by my therapist.

As graduation neared, I'd developed anxiety — not about finding a job, but about my lack of dates. "I feel like I've wasted the past four years," I told the on-campus therapist, who I could meet with for free in my remaining months as a student. Despite being surrounded by nice Christian boys, the kind I was supposed to marry, I had yet to go on a first date. My shyness, I told her, was to blame.

She sent me out of her office with a few extra Kleenex and a homework assignment: Strike up a conversation with a stranger at Starbucks. I knew her intentions were good, but coming up with conversation starters for a coffee shop made me feel sad and incapable.

This is why I decided to modify the assignment. Instead of going to Starbucks, I knocked on my

10

neighbors' open door and said, "Hi, I'm Dani. I've seen you guys a bit—I live just across the sidewalk—and wanted to say hi."

I was formal and buttoned-up, and they were way too cool for me, slumped, holding cans of cheap beer, and shirtless. I'd done my deed, so I was ready to run back into hiding. And then they offered me a beer.

Drinking was just one of the many things that could get a student expelled from my Christian college, because all students were required to sign "The Covenant," a contract that outlined the school's expected Christian lifestyle: no drinking, no premarital sex, no smoking. Unlike the Christian colleges my friends attended, we didn't get a break on holiday weekends or after we turned 21: drinking was off-limits for all students, staff, and faculty.

Still, it was senior year, and I didn't want to be rude, so I took the beer.

It wasn't my first drink. My first taste of alcohol was a shot of Patron at a bar in Pacific Beach. It was my former roommate Jennifer's twenty-first birthday; I was almost twenty-two. On my own twenty-first birthday, I had ordered a Shirley Temple, not wanting my friends to judge me or, worse, report me to the school authorities.

By the time I had beer with my neighbors, I was familiar with drinking, so I drank slowly, not wanting to get drunk.

My roommates got home much later to find my pants and underwear on the floor by the closet, topped by my shirt and bra, as if I had been standing there and disappeared out of them.

"We thought we missed the Rapture, and you had been taken!" they told me, referencing an evangelical Christian belief that God will one day sweep all true believers up to meet him in the sky and all others will be stuck on Earth to live through the "end times," leading up to final demolishment of the world.

The truth was, after the beer, I'd run home to change into my bathing suit to go to the apartment complex's hot tub with my new neighbor friends.

Rebellion wasn't new to me. My high school years were defined by trying to get spaghetti strap tops past my mom and lying when I went to a movie I wasn't allowed to see. Despite this, I found myself being the "good kid" in many social circles. At church, I was less interested in makeup and boys than the other girls, and when I got bored during services, I'd flip to a random page in the Old Testament and read wild stories about kings and prophets. My silence was accepted as model behavior. My self-control made me superior, and the rules were a route to my reward, like getting dessert after eating your healthy dinner. I imagined that as I developed spiritually, with regular prayer, reading my Bible, and leading a pure lifestyle, I would be attractive to the right kind of men and would wind up marrying a hot pastor. But by the end of college, I was doubting the fantasy would come true the way I had expected.

I went back the following evening. After another round of the hot tub and cheap beers, we watched a video of a fight Bryan narrowly lost in Thailand as his roommate provided gushing commentary. Bryan had blond hair and blue eyes; perfect, clear skin; and the body of a Ken doll—more muscular than the guys I usually liked, but at the same time, his toned body gave me the illusion I had walked into a magazine.

After the fight was over, we switched to music, and Bryan's roommate headed back to his room. Bryan finally kissed me. This whole time I'd been wondering if he liked me, or if I was just another person to hang out with, and finally I had my proof: He found me attractive. I hoped he couldn't tell how inexperienced I was—my first kiss was just a few months earlier, almost by accident, when I danced with a tall and dashing stranger at the Hard Rock Cafe on New Year's.

Bryan went to the kitchen, and I decided to head home, because I was bored, but also because my roommates and I all slept on two bunk beds in one room, and they'd notice if I got in late.

As Christians, we were all committed to waiting until we were married to have sex, and the last thing I needed was a lecture from my friends about spending too much time in a boy's apartment, which could lead to that thing we were supposed to avoid. I wouldn't tell them about the kissing. For someone who had never dated, I was making real progress in addressing my shyness, and was willing to make some compromises to ensure I wasn't forever single.

I went to the kitchen and told Bryan I was leaving, and gave him a hug. The hug lasted longer than I expected, and then he took my hand and slid it down into his sweatpants, and wrapped my fingers around his slack penis. Then he slowly dragged my hand up, leaving his penis poking out of the top of his pants.

I'd never seen a penis, unless you count pictures of the statue of David in textbooks, much less touched one. After years of expecting my first sexual experience to be with my husband, I wasn't sure what I lost by touching Bryan's penis. Would I have to tell my husband that I did this, as part of an admission of previous sexual activities? It wasn't intentional—he grabbed my hand without asking.

I pulled my hand away. Mostly speechless, I stammered, "Good night," and left.

Safely back in my top bunk bed, with my roommates around me already sleeping, I lay awake, thinking. I'd expected a penis to feel more . . . magical? So much of my upbringing told me that drinking alcohol and being alone with a guy would inevitably lead to sex, but I'd proved them wrong. Plus, I'd hung out with a boy, despite my shyness!

This probably wouldn't lead to dating, because Bryan was not a Christian and did not have the same "values"—which is the Christian way of saying he wasn't waiting until marriage for sex. Touching Bryan was probably OK, because I didn't do it on purpose.

He was really attractive and talented, and seemed to like me, which was flattering.

It's a little weird he didn't even try to sleep with me, I thought.

FOREPLAY

Years later, it occurred to me that he did try to sleep with me. That he didn't put my hand on his penis because he thought I'd enjoy it, as I had assumed, but because it felt good to him.

At the time, it was completely lost on me that Bryan was trying to engage in foreplay. I had no idea what foreplay even was; that word didn't enter my vocabulary until I rented The Holiday. In the movie, a drunk Jude Law asks Cameron Diaz, "How do you feel about foreplay?"

"Overrated," she responds, and then they have sex.

So "fore" likely means "before," and I understood the meaning of "play"—so in tying foreplay to sex, it would mean the "play" that came before sex. Previously, I assumed two people would just say, "Let's have sex," and go directly to intercourse.

I've since learned that such pre-sex activities can help with arousal, which makes the vaginal opening sensitive and moist, or "wet," and the penis erect. I wasn't aroused with Bryan.

Bryan wasn't that aroused, either—his penis was still slack when I touched it, but he'd clearly been hoping I'd help him get hard.

Years after the experience with Bryan, I read a book called How to Be a Great Lover and tried to practice giving a hand job with a banana, but got lost on thumb direction and hand movement because I was imagining a penis pointing down instead of up.

Since I wasn't allowed to see PG-13 movies and didn't have cable TV, I was never exposed to sex scenes or innuendo, so I missed learning about foreplay, getting wet, and handjobs. My friends were all

Christians. The health class at my public junior high school (in overwhelmingly conservative Orange County) had a few sessions related to sex, but students had to get their parents to sign a permission slip to attend—and my parents opted me out.

I knew women could have orgasms, because I had seen When Harry Met Sally, which features a famous scene when Meg Ryan fakes an orgasm in a diner. But I was well into my twenties before I found out women could masturbate and have an orgasm alone. I must have thought the penis came with pixie dust—it didn't occur to me that sex is pleasurable for women because the female body itself contains nerve endings (which can be activated by a finger, or a hot tub jet, or the stream of a bathtub spout, or a marshmallow, or a pickle, to name just a few good options).

I didn't have sex with Bryan that night because I didn't know he was initiating it. But I also wanted to first have that experience with my husband—the man God picked out specifically for me. Sex unites people, and although Bryan was cute, he wasn't the person I wanted to be with permanently.

It didn't matter that people in movies and TV

shows were having sex, or that it was common for non-Christians. "For the word of the cross is foolishness to those who are perishing," the Bible reads (1 Corinthians 1:18). I knew Christians were right to wait.

MODESTY

Though California is a liberal state, I grew up in the region that vehemently campaigned to prevent same-sex marriage from becoming legal in 2008. And among churches in Orange County, mine was one of the most conservative.

Calvary Chapel is part of an association of churches operating under the same name. It started in Costa Mesa, California, in the 1960s with the "Jesus movement," a trend characterized by the inclusion of drums in religious music (sacrilegious at the time) and a focus on evangelizing and reading the Bible literally, as early first-century Christians would have, without interpretation from a Bible scholar.

By 2000, when I was going through puberty and coming of age, my church in the southern California suburbs was markedly less "hippie" and was something of a white, middle-class social club. We had pizza at youth group and a midweek Bible study for junior high and high school students. Every second Sunday of the month, there was a potluck after church, and every fourth Saturday, church members headed to the local abortion clinic to protest.

I identified with this type of activism and the perceived alienation; it was part of being a Christian. I listened exclusively to Christian music, especially a band called DC Talk and its hit song "Jesus Freak," identifying with the line that defiantly boasts of the Christian faith, "What will people do / when they find out it's true?"—knowing the implication was that when these non-Christians did find out "it" was true (that you needed to give your life to Jesus to be saved), it might be too late and they'd be in hell.

I never made it to the abortion protests, but I did raise money for Christian hunger relief organizations and handed out "tracts"—small pamphlets that explain how to get to heaven—to strangers out for dinner in downtown Laguna Beach on a Saturday night.

At school, I hung out with Christian friends who went to other, similar churches and whose parents wouldn't allow them to watch the same movies. I preferred this. In grade school, when a parent at a sleepover turned on a PG-13 movie, The Mask, I called my mom, asking her to pick me up because I was scared, but also because I knew I wasn't allowed to watch it. Having friends who followed similar rules meant I didn't have to constantly be on guard. In high school, when I did a class project with a classmate and found out she was an atheist, I realized that even though I liked her, I felt conflicted in pursuing a friendship with someone who wouldn't go to heaven.

Still, I was fascinated by those people who were free from the rules and restrictions that defined me. When I joined the swim team, I buddied up with a couple girls sitting out practice in the locker room, where the male swim coach couldn't find us.

"Are you guys excited about prom?" Allie asked Rula, referencing Rula's longtime boyfriend.

"Yeah, except I'm going to be on my period," she said.

"You still think you'll hook up?" another girl asked.

"Probably," she said, laughing, and everyone accepted her answer as reasonable.

Would I have sex on my period after I was married? It sounded messy. Plus, I was surprised at how openly Rula admitted she was sleeping with her boyfriend. If they were going to do it while she was on her period, it probably wasn't going to be their first time.

I hoped no one would ask me if I was going to prom, much less if I planned to have sex. I had crushes but didn't talk to boys, unless it was part of a class assignment. Often the girls would try to be inclusive and ask me questions if I wasn't speaking up, but when it came to the topic of romance, I prayed they'd skip over me.

I knew that if I did say anything about boys, I'd have to set a good example by telling them I was waiting until marriage for sex. It was my responsibility to share my faith with others in hopes it would save them from hell, so I felt guilty by staying silent, but their stories gave me a voyeuristic look into a lifestyle I would never experience.

While I had no intention of dating the boys at my public school like these girls could, I still wanted the boys to like me, and saw my appearance as the solution.

This brought tension at home. Once, I burst into tears, standing in front of the dressing room mirror at Charlotte Russe, wearing a beige mock turtleneck tank top that made me look tan and brought out the blonde in my hair. It would never be mine.

"It's skin-tight," my mom said, saying the words as if they meant the shirt was woven with poisonous snake venom. "If you lift up your arms it will show your entire stomach. Your top needs to overlap your jeans by at least two inches." I wasn't convinced.

"You don't want to attract the wrong kind of attention," she explained.

I did, though. I imagined myself wearing that shirt to class and finally ceasing to be invisible. Maybe the guys would check me out or start a conversation. Maybe the popular girls would want to be my friend.

My family rules did provide one benefit—they

shielded me from breaking the rules at my church.

At church outings to the beach or to summer camp, girls were not allowed to wear a two-piece swimsuit—and if they did, they had to wear board shorts and a shirt on top of it. I only owned a one-piece and didn't need to worry about wearing board shorts, but as soon as I realized I was the only girl my age without a bikini, I talked my mom into letting me get a two-piece and board shorts—specifically to be worn with a shirt on top, to fit in.

Showing too much skin, the church leaders said, would "cause the boys to stumble," or sin. Sin wasn't just an action—it could be thoughts as well. Men can't help but have illicit thoughts when they see too much of a woman's body, so to be respectful of our "Christian brothers," we should dress modestly—essentially clearing the boys of any guilt and passing the shame onto the girls and their bodies.

When a younger girl said she couldn't sit down at youth group because her skirt was too short, the leaders made an example of her the following week, not naming her, but reiterating the situation to underline why there were guidelines around church attire. How embarrassing, I thought, relieved my parents' rules protected me from making such a horrible mistake.

Even though I knew thoughts could be sinful, I still fantasized about having sex with my church crush, the tall lanky lead guitar player in the church band, but because I didn't talk to boys, nothing ever happened. Since my fantasies featured sex outside of marriage, I assumed they were a sin, too, so I prayed that I could stop—but it was hard to control my thoughts. When I got older, I started saying no to my crush in the fantasies—before we inevitably still had sex—because at least then, I wasn't daydreaming about willingly taking part in sin, although it didn't seem like a very good solution to fantasize about my crush as a perpetrator of rape.

"If you're drinking, or doing drugs, or having sex, you are NOT a Christian!" our youth pastor would declare, his voice raised, during especially passionate parts of his Sunday sermon to junior high and high school students. I wondered if any of my fellow churchgoers were actually drinking or having sex, or if the youth pastor was trying to atone for his own pre-conversion behavior.

There was also a communal aspect to the sex

rule. It signified to me who was really in or out of the Christian faith.

At my first job in the Macy's juniors department, on the second floor of a quiet mall across the street from a retirement community, I worked with a high school classmate. Tracy and I bonded the day we decided the mannequins needed to be restyled. We figured out how to pull off the arms as we removed a mannequin's blouse and skirt, then pulled the torso off the leg that was attached to the base. But, as we started to pull off the other leg, wanting to dress her in jeans, we realized it was stuck. With my arms around the torso and Tracy gripping the leg, we faced each other like kids playing tug-of-war and each leaned back, forcing all our human strength into the mannequin. After a few tries we were crying with laughter, desperate to finish the job. After that day, I saw Tracy as a friend, not just a coworker.

I was sad when Tracy told me she lost her virginity.

"He was helping me study, and he told me I could have a kiss for every flashcard I got right," she said, grinning as she explained what led to her hookup with the guy from community college. I was finishing my senior year of high school, and Tracy was a year older.

"How was it?" I asked, trying to mask my despair but not wanting to deprive her of the chance to talk about the sensitive memory. I was also flattered she trusted me with it.

"It was good," Tracy said, not needing to say more.

She was a Christian, but not devout. I wished I had been able to warn her of the consequences, but now it was too late.

One day, around the holidays, my sister, Katie, came home from lunch with a couple from our church group who had moved and were back in town for the week.

"They told us they weren't pure when they got married," Katie said, recounting the conversations of the day. I wondered if they felt they needed to do a round of confessions since Peter, the husband, wanted to be a pastor. I remembered their wedding, at church, the bride wearing a full, lacey white dress. It was no wonder they felt the need to confess later, I thought. The whole wedding was a lie.

A friend once told me a girl at her church had to

get up in front of the congregation to apologize after she got pregnant outside of marriage. When one of my former college roommates moved in with her boyfriend in between apartments, I felt she had wronged me personally. Not having sex until marriage is so countercultural, there's a sense that as Christians, we're in it together—as long as your friends are holding out, you know you can do it, too.

CONSEQUENCES

The youth group at my church met in a converted office building next to the church building, all inside a business district across the street from Jack in the Box and within walking distance of Sonshine Christian Bookstore. Once we were junior high age, we'd start Sunday mornings in the main sanctuary for worship music, then leave after announcements for a more age-appropriate sermon from our youth pastor.

Along with our youth pastor, we were led by volunteers—some older teens and a couple who became Christians after they were married, and had thus left behind their life of sin, but still had tattoos and an affinity for motorcycles that made them edgy in our suburban, upper-middle-class church.

It was for that reason that, after church one day when I was in high school, I tagged along when I heard another student asking Eric, the husband, why it was so important to wait until marriage for sex. Eric was among only a few people I knew who had life experience outside these sharply drawn lines. He should know.

"Picture the most beautiful mountain range you can imagine—the Rockies!" he said, rubbing his chin and pulling at his long beard. "That's what sex is like for me and Amber."

"Now, think of the Garden of Eden, with beauty so unreal we on earth can't even picture what it was like—that's what sex is when it's done as God intended," he explained.

God just wants us to have better sex, I concluded. I was OK with that.

At another church, when I was in my twenties, the pastor discussed a study on sexual satisfaction.

"Christian women have the most satisfying sex,

this study found," he said. "That's not surprising to me. The couples I've done premarital counseling with—and I've met with a lot of Christian couples— they say their only regret is they wished they had saved more for marriage, not less."

I wondered if holding out on kissing until my wedding day would result in the best possible sex.

A local event featuring Christian bands and a celebrity pastor further built my case for waiting until marriage. Protection, the pastor said, only works 70 percent of the time—so sex is like being handed a parachute that's 70 percent reliable and jumping out of an airplane (as if pregnancy or disease is equivalent to death). Because I had never learned about sexually transmitted diseases—they're irrelevant if you and your partner will only ever be with each other—I figured he was telling the truth.

Sex is a beautiful thing designed for a husband and wife inside marriage, I learned. But the more I was told about sex, the more it seemed to carry a dark side.

"Once boys hit puberty, all they care about is sex," a friend's mom said from the front of her minivan, driving a group of us home from school. "They'll say anything they need to get you in bed." I glanced over at my friend's younger brother, maybe 13, and hoped this wasn't true of Christian boys, too.

The celebrity pastor at the event knew it would be hard for us to resist sex, and taught us a few talking points for dealing with common situations.

"If your boyfriend says, 'if you love me, you'll have sex with me,' you say, 'If you love me, you'd support me in waiting.' "

"If he says, 'But I just can't control myself around you!' you say, 'If you can't control yourself around me now, how will you control yourself with other women after we are married?' "

These phrases were intended to be helpful and empower young women in upholding their life choices. But as a girl who did not have a boyfriend and had not been invited to have sex, I internalized that if a guy wanted to have sex with me, it meant he didn't love me and would probably cheat on me later. This would come back to haunt me.

CHRISTIAN COLLEGE

Point Loma was a small private school on a hill overlooking the ocean. It had its own subculture. Because the school belonged to the Nazarene denomination, we could not put on a school-sponsored dance, as the denomination considered it morally wanting. But at the same time, my mom considered the school to be liberal because the science department taught evolution. Because the lower dorms are walkable to the waves, the school attracted a fair number of students with little interest in faith.

My parents agreed to allow me to go away to a four-year college, instead of living at home and attending community college, only if I chose a Christian school. I knew Point Loma required students to abide by the Covenant, but I didn't drink, smoke, or plan on having sex, so I wasn't concerned with those rules. Even inside those rules, being away from home would give me more leniency. Finally, I'd be able to watch a movie without my parents' DVD player muting out the swear words.

My rebel side wasn't let down. Within the first few weeks of school, my dorm's resident assistant told the girls on our hall about a school tradition called "nossing," which is an acronym for "naked ocean swimming."

After midnight, we piled into cars and drove to nearby Coronado Beach, which was remote enough to limit the possibility of running into anyone else, but also had calm waves we could safely jump into in the dark. The sophomores in the group advised us to wear shorts and a zip-up hoodie, because they were easy to pull off and back on.

We whispered as we carefully walked in a herd down the sand, stopping close to the water. Once we agreed it was time, all twenty of us dropped our clothes, and immediately we were shrieking and laughing, struggling to recognize each other's faces in the dark while giggling, "Look how cute you are," as we admired each other's bodies.

"Who says Christians can't have fun," I bragged to Christian friends who went to other Christian colleges. It was better than skinny-dipping—because it was women-only, there was no lust involved.

As I got in the rhythm of college life, I fell into the more conservative cliques, volunteering to lead on-campus Bible studies and going on mission trips, a sort of humanitarian summer vacation in partnership with local churches around the world.

These groups, however pious, didn't take themselves too seriously and poked fun at purity culture. "We were going to do the Parable of the 10 Virgins, but we didn't have enough," a girl said in a skit, glancing backwards at another girl, who shamefully looked at the ground. This was all part of the skit, meant to portray the worst possible blunders so we could avoid making these mistakes when representing the school at churches in Tanzania, the Dominican Republic, or El Salvador.

I marveled at the girl who had offered to play the part of the non-virgin. I supposed it wouldn't be funny if she was actually not a virgin. Since we had all signed the pledge to not take part in premarital sex, we were free to laugh about it.

I never doubted some students were breaking the Covenant. Some of my fellow Bible study leaders agreed that drinking alcohol was not inherently sinful, but signing the Covenant and then breaking it counted as lying, which was a sin. If you found out someone in your dorm was drinking and you didn't turn them in, you were lying, too. This created a tense culture. There was little acknowledgment that students went to off-campus parties with drinking or even sex and drugs.

In a memorable crack in our façade, a school newspaper op-ed once referenced students driving down to Mexico, over the border, and two students having sex in the back seat of a car on the way back. I was shocked that such activities actually existed underneath the surface.

BIBLE READING

At Point Loma, students were required to take three religion classes, no matter their major. One of them was a class on the Old Testament, which I took second semester of my freshman year. My professor was also a pastor at a local church, and he used to joke, "Bible classes should have labs the way the science department does—but this would make the animal sacrifice portions of the Bible especially messy to teach." I laughed at the mental picture of students scrambling around on the school's carefully manicured lawns, trying to light an altar on fire after slaughtering a goat.

Our first class reading was from the study Bible that was the assigned class textbook—an essay that discussed the "myth" of Adam and Eve. In fact, it described everything that took place before the Flood as myth. Why would they put an essay written by an atheist in a Bible? I wondered. Months later I realized the science department teaching evolution wasn't a compromise with secular culture, but consistent with how the religious studies department taught the Bible.

The following fall, I took the New Testament class. My professor in this class continued to challenge beliefs I took as fact from my longtime church.

"The word 'virgin' in the Old Testament means 'young woman,' " he said, referencing prophecies that said the messiah would be born to a virgin, and used by Christians to back up the claim that Jesus' mother, Mary, was a virgin when she gave birth to him. "The word has nothing to do with sexual status."

The applications of this were perplexing! If Jesus was conceived in a biological way just like the rest of us, could he still be God? At the same time, it seemed to not matter at all. One thing my Christian college taught me was that many Christians believe many different things, and what I learned in church growing up was just one version.

Questioning the translation of the word "virgin" was a splinter into my Christian worldview. If something like the virgin birth—so central to my beliefs—could be wrong, perhaps I was wrong about other things, too.

"What were Jesus's last words?" the New Testament professor would ask our class. The four Gospels don't agree, breaking my literal and historically accurate interpretation of the Bible.

By the time I got to an ethics class my senior year, I was comfortable challenging long-held beliefs. I went back to all the verses I had ever associated with Christian purity, and dug up translations to see if I could gain some clarity.

In the Old Testament, marriage is described as a business transaction in which women did not have consent, so virginity is highlighted as a matter of monetary value, not morals.

New Testament verses 1 Corinthians 6:9, 2 Corinthians 12:21, Galatians 5:19, and Hebrews 13:4[1] are the ones I most often heard in church to condemn premarital sex. They reference impurity and sexual immorality, translated as fornication from the Greek word "porneia." The word actually refers to slaves being sold for temple prostitution, which could easily be a condemnation of worshipping other gods, not sex acts.

Genesis 2:23–25, also quoted in Mark 10:6–9 and 1 Corinthians 6:16[2], says that when a man and woman

---

1 1 Corinthians 6:9

Or do you not know that wrongdoers will not inherit the kingdom of God? Do not be deceived: Neither the sexually immoral nor idolaters nor adulterers nor men who have sex with men . . .

2 Corinthians 12:21

I am afraid that when I come again my God will humble me before you, and I will be grieved over many who have sinned earlier and have not repented of the impurity, sexual sin and debauchery in which they have indulged.

Galatians 5:19

The acts of the flesh are obvious: sexual immorality, impurity and debauchery;

Hebrews 13:4

Marriage should be honored by all, and the marriage bed kept pure, for God will judge the adulterer and all the sexually immoral.

2 Genesis 2: 23-25

23 The man said,

"This is now bone of my bones

and flesh of my flesh;

she shall be called 'woman,'

are married, they become one flesh. I returned to this verse when I had doubts about the purpose of waiting until marriage for sex. Two becoming one flesh sounds pretty permanent, and is perhaps what I inferred to be so binding about sex (and terrifying about uniting oneself with the wrong person). Here was a union that could only be broken through death.

For my final essay in my ethics class, I decided to go against my own beliefs and write in support of allowing premarital sex for Christians. I wondered if I could make the case for it, as an intellectual exercise.

My main points included that the rule was originally set to protect women—in the patriarchal culture the Bible was written, women could not own

for she was taken out of man."

24 That is why a man leaves his father and mother and is united to his wife, and they become one flesh.

25 Adam and his wife were both naked, and they felt no shame.

Mark 10:6-9

6 "But from the beginning of creation, God MADE THEM MALE AND FEMALE. 7 "for this reason a man shall leave his father and mother, 8 and the two shall become one flesh; so they are no longer two, but one flesh. 9 What therefore God has joined together, let no man separate."

1 Corinthians 6:16

Do you not know that he who unites himself with a prostitute is one with her in body? For it is said, "The two will become one flesh."

property, so how could they care for children without a husband? There was no protection, so STDs would be passed more freely. The average marriage age has since increased. Was God's intent that a woman today who remains single into her thirties (or later) remain abstinent well into her adult life?

I turned in the essay, unsure if my professor would grade it low and write a comment on it accusing me of being impure with the boyfriend I didn't have, or turn me into school authorities. He did none of these things. I got an A.

Not every academic department at Point Loma was so open-minded. In at least one case, modern science was used to endorse traditional Christian morals.

As a business major at a school that advocated for abstinence until marriage, I took one science class and didn't learn much about the human body to compensate for the sex education I still lacked. I knew sex could lead to pregnancy, but still wasn't sure of the specifics. But my friend Julie, who was studying psychology, learned some things about the brain relevant to our faith, and eagerly shared with me one day at Starbucks.

"Dani," she said, "I think I want to be a sex therapist!"

I glanced over at a man working on his computer, who was silently chuckling.

"When you have sex, the brain releases chemicals which, for the woman, cause her to trust the man she is with, but for the man, they cause him to feel a sort of ownership or responsibility to protect the woman," she said.

"Wow, that's so interesting," I said, noting that her explanation fit with pop culture, where movies were always showing women getting attached and men sleeping around, and neither able to resist developing feelings if they repeatedly slept together.

Years later, I did my own research on oxytocin, and realized what she explained to me was a simplistic and perhaps sexist understanding of the chemical.[3]

---

3 Oxytocin is a chemical that, along with dopamine, is released during not just sexual intercourse but all kinds of intimacy, including holding hands, daydreaming about someone, and eye contact, both with humans and pets (Macdonald 2010).

Oxytocin is naturally released during labor and breastfeeding, and can be used as a drug to induce labor. While it has garnered the nickname "the love hormone," the definition is often misleading.

For example, in studies of small mice-like animals called prairie voles, it was found that virgin (i.e., childless) voles would exhibit maternal behavior in responding to

But the seed was planted. I left Starbucks that day believing that sex could infiltrate my brain and turn my body against me, making me "trust" any person I might sleep with.

---

crying baby voles if they were exposed to oxytocin. However, it doesn't follow that oxytocin caused the voles to care about these babies. A researcher described the effect to me as "social salience." Oxytocin does not create feelings; it heightens awareness to social cues.

Another study, of humans, found that men in relationships given a spray of oxytocin stood further away from attractive women than men not given oxytocin (and oxytocin had no effect on single men), suggesting oxytocin can promote faithfulness (Deutschländer 2011). Again, not passing morals or value judgments, just surfacing the inherent values of the subjects.

Far from being something that would cause us to have feelings, oxytocin appears to enhance what already exists. The effects of oxytocin can last a few hours.

51

SECULAR LIVING

When I graduated from college, I briefly planned to move overseas to be a missionary, hopefully in Sub-Saharan Africa, where I had gone on a missions trip. Instead, the organization I worked with matched me with a missionary in Italy, and midway through raising money for a year abroad, the cost and difficulties in getting a long-term visa made the adventure not worth the effort.

By the time I realized I had nowhere to go, my lease with my college classmates had almost expired.

Wanting to avoid moving home at all costs, I calculated what my part-time job at a coffee shop was paying me and found an apartment on Craigslist, where I would share a one-bedroom apartment with another girl.

It would be my first experience living with a non-Christian, a fact I downplayed when I talked to family and friends but secretly found exciting. All my life I had been taught to share my faith with non-Christians, but I hadn't had friendships deep enough to feel comfortable talking about faith. I wondered if what I was told was true—that my new roommate would, over time, admire my superior lifestyle and want to hear more about Jesus.

Mary was from upstate New York and liked to "party," something I was unfamiliar with, as I had always understood a "party" to be an event one could attend, not a verb. The friend she'd moved out to California with had bailed, so the other half of the room was open, and we soon realized neither of us had any experience living with someone we didn't already know.

"I thought your bed would be bigger," she said, when I set up my Ikea twin bed. "I was going to hang a curtain from the ceiling but I guess we don't need to."

She motioned to the few feet of carpet between my bed and her queen-sized mattress sitting on top of a box spring on the floor. At first I didn't understand why a curtain would be needed, having shared a room with other girls for many years, but I would soon learn.

The move itself took a couple days, with my bed being one of the last things I moved to the new place. But my former roommates and I, adamant that we get our security deposit back from the apartment complex, stayed up until 2:00 a.m. cleaning. When I arrived at the new place to sleep for the first night, I carefully opened the door, hoping to not wake my new roommate.

"Fuck, fuck, fuck," I heard coming from the kitchen. "Jesus Christ," a softer voice said. I could hear some slurping noises and, despite my innocence, recognized these as the sounds of sex.

The sounds continued, and I backed up and closed the metal door just as quietly. I slowly walked in the cool night air the two blocks to the Ocean Beach pier. Had I made a horrible mistake? The stars and the moon didn't offer answers. I loved that I lived this close to the beach, that I could walk down to the water anytime I wanted. But I didn't like the circumstances.

The social implications of walking in on a roommate having sex were new to me. Was I supposed to go elsewhere? Should she be embarrassed?

After some thought, I decided to go home, this time rattling the metal security door as I unlocked it. The tactic worked, and the couple ran into the bathroom. I was relieved that I wouldn't have to sleep on one of the loveseat-sized couches in our living room, but perturbed that I now couldn't brush my teeth. But then, after I shut the bedroom door, I heard them both leave, and I had the place to myself.

"I want to be a cool girl," Mary told me one night when we went out drinking together at the neighborhood Irish pub. The guy she'd been sleeping with had been hanging out with another girl who her friend group perceived as trashy because she worked as a stripper. Mary didn't want to appear jealous, because she and the guy weren't officially dating. A "cool girl" wouldn't get attached or possessive of a guy she was sleeping with, brain hormones be damned.

What she said confirmed for me what Julie told me that day in Starbucks: Sex is different for women than it is for men. Women who have sex are forced to pretend they don't have emotions, when emotions, and the capacity to care for another person, are wonderful things. Men did not have these emotions, it seemed. I was glad I wasn't having sex.

I didn't openly criticize others for having sex, but I could see that their relationships were destructive. The "evangelical" part of my religion that said I should convert others was fading. Instead, I hoped that by living alongside them, I could set an example that would be an invitation to a better life. In the meantime, just like those girls on the swim team, I wanted to observe their lives, watching for affirmation that waiting on sex was the best thing to do.

The apartment dynamic shifted when another of Mary's friends from New York moved in. "Our rent will be really cheap," she told me, as if that made three girls living together in a one-bedroom more palatable. Meanwhile, my friend Laura, from yoga, was getting ready to move, and the cost to share the master bedroom of a house with her was the same as I was already paying, so I gave Mary my thirty days' notice and moved in with Laura.

Less than a week after we moved in, with Laura's former roommate Lisa and her boyfriend in the second room and Jeff from Craigslist filling the third room, Laura's boyfriend Jason got robbed in his own apartment, and he moved in, too. Suddenly, I was sharing a bedroom with a couple.

"Just don't have sex while I'm in the room," I told Laura, tired of feeling like a third wheel in my own home when my previous roommate had guests over.

There were six roommates total in the house, and we'd spend late nights drinking wine together in the living room, listening to music because we didn't pay for cable, and talking.

"Dani's still a virgin," Laura announced one night with genuine affection. "I think it's sweet!"

"Most of my friends are, too," I said in defense of myself. "I want to save my first time for my husband."

"That's cool," another roommate said. After years of thinking non-Christians would judge me as I had judged them, I was relieved to not have to explain my choice.

That year, a longtime friend of Jason's stopped by our house and went on a long walk around the neighborhood with him. Upon returning, Jason told me how she was waiting for a much older guy she was in love with to choose between her and the woman he had a baby with.

"Maybe it is better to just not have sex," Jason told me when he returned, frustrated by the impossible situation this girl had gotten herself into. Even Jason, an atheist, could recognize that intimacy came with consequences.

Despite other people's sexual failures, Laura and Jason were the perfect foil to my belief that sex before marriage was bad for relationships. They met as coworkers at an electronics store and started hooking up, which led to dating. They had a great relationship, the kind I dreamed of having, and it had started with . . . casual sex.

Meanwhile, I didn't have a boyfriend. Non-Christian guys were off-limits to date because they might want to have sex, and I would have to say no. My only options were the guys at church, a much smaller pool. I joined midweek small groups at church and signed up to volunteer at church events, but still came up empty. Finding a Christian guy was my preference, but I was starting to wonder if God had preordained me to be single.

The more I waited for my secular friends'

relationships to fail, the more I saw positive examples of relationships that were intimate, but not destructive.

Just over a year after graduating from college, I moved to Chicago for graduate school. In lieu of settling down with the hot pastor I had imagined, I was beginning to see my career in journalism as my most worthy pursuit. But I was still hoping God would bring the right future spouse into my life at the right time. The purpose of dating was marriage, so I didn't bother with a date if I didn't see marriage potential.

In Chicago, I moved, sight unseen, into a five-bedroom apartment that was the lower unit of a brownstone, encompassing the first floor and basement. The apartment was a mile from Northwestern University's campus, and my roommates were also graduate students: three in mathematics and one in neuroscience. They were all male.

Just like when I first lived with a non-Christian, I downplayed this fact. My mom once warned me that sleeping under the same roof with a guy would put a person at risk of having sex—you'd be up late one night watching TV, and inevitably someone would make a move. After living with guys already, I doubted this was true. Besides, I trusted my own self-control—and the rent was really cheap.

By graduate school at age 23, I was just starting to unravel how my body worked. I had discovered masturbating while house-sitting, before moving to Chicago for graduate school. The house had a hot tub, and while I had heard of a girl using a banana to mimic sex, I didn't want to put a physical object in my vagina, fearing it would get stuck. It occurred to me that I could point the hot tub jets at my vagina. I discovered I could cause an interesting sensation with this act, but did not think it constituted an orgasm.

Later, while in graduate school and living alone in a studio apartment, I figured out how to reach orgasm with the bathtub faucet and later with my finger. I read in a Christian book that masturbation was not OK. But I wasn't thinking about a specific person when I was masturbating, so in my mind it wasn't lust. Plus, I wondered if I was doing my future husband a favor by figuring out my body.

One of my roommates was dating an undergraduate girl he met through the school's hiking club. "Do you know how to make an omelette?" she asked him one morning as they rattled pans and silverware in the kitchen right outside my room. I saw him kiss her neck as I walked to the bathroom. I was embarrassed to observe the intimacy, but also fascinated to see what it was like to have a steady boyfriend up close.

They weren't the wild, drunken couple I walked in on my first night at the new apartment in San Diego. What they did wasn't the promiscuity I had been warned about in church—it was respectful, loving, committed intimacy. But they also weren't going to get married. After she graduated from college, she moved across the country for her own graduate program.

When I thought about them, I wondered about oxytocin. I wondered if it was harder for them to break up, when the time came, than it would have been, had they not been spending nights together. Then, I wondered if all those Saturdays they woke up late together and cooked omelettes made the heartbreak worth it.

They didn't get pregnant or suffer any of the other consequences I had been taught would come with unmarried sex. It seemed like they could move on emotionally, become happily married to other people, and always carry the positive memory of their time as a couple in Chicago.

The only missing piece was God's blessing, and the Eden-level sex that I believed came with following the rules in the Bible—but even that was beginning to sound suspect.

GOD

Most Christians agree that the Bible requires some interpretation. Historically, before Martin Luther wrote his 95 Theses, Christians had to trust what Catholic priests told them about God because the priests read the Bible in Latin and it was not translated into everyday language. When Protestantism arose, any Christian could read the Bible themselves, and the split instigated this change in the Catholic church, too.

I was part of a Bible study group in college that was intent on taking the Bible literally, fearing it would lose its meaning if we wrote off this or that section—being culturally relevant wasn't Christian; Christianity was supposed to be countercultural. Churches I attended pressed a similar view by saying that anyone should be able to read a Bible and understand God's intentions.

But as I further studied the Bible, read more about its origins, and learned about apparent contradictions such as Jesus' last words, I determined that it did need interpretation and to be understood within cultural context. I could no longer read "avoid sexual immorality" and assume that meant intercourse before marriage. I also couldn't take at face value the verses that condemn same-sex intimacy.

Interpretation or not, the Bible was written in different languages, and the translation of individual words requires an understanding of the culture at the time. Choosing the appropriate translated word requires making some assumptions about today's culture. A section in the New Testament that admonishes women to not wear their hair braided is generally not taken literally, but interpreted to mean women should not be obsessed with outward appearance. The words may refer to braids, but the intent, translated across cultures, is vanity. Many Christians describe this type of interpretation as understanding the spirit, not the letter, of the law.

Understanding what "the law" is, and what God intended for us, comes back to who God is. I was always taught that God loves us, and that the rules, or laws, in the Bible, were written to protect us, so we could live life to the fullest[4]. On the surface this seems congruent, but in my spiritual life I was plagued by the idea that God didn't really love me.

I'd heard that sometimes if a person has an abusive parent, it's hard to believe God is loving, because their own parent was not. This didn't add up for me; my parents were nothing short of caring. It was strange that I questioned this truth so central to my faith.

One fear remained stuck in my mind. In the Bible, Paul writes that it is better to remain single[5], and I'd often heard the verse explained that God calls some

---

4 John 10:10: The thief comes only to steal and kill and destroy; I have come that they may have life, and have it to the full.

5 1 Corinthians 7:8: Now to the unmarried[a] and the widows I say: It is good for them to stay unmarried, as I do.

people to never be married, and instead focus on God's work. I wondered if it was God's plan to exclude me from marriage, and it seemed such a God did not want me to be happy.

I could fathom a life of being unmarried, but couldn't deal with a life cut off from all intimate relationships. Movies and songs may be entertainment, but they also reflect our deepest human needs and desires, and most of them are about love. How could a loving God want to exclude me from this?

In order to continue believing in a loving God, I had to reject this understanding of God—this vindictive God who would punish, whose love was actually conditional. If a marriage could suffer because of premarital sex, the sin wasn't really forgiven. I replaced this view with a God who interacts with us humans only with mercy and never with shame.

Imagine a kid who, while roller-skating down a hill a little too fast, falls and scrapes her knee. A loving parent would clean the wound and comfort her. In the same way, a loving God, when presented with a heartbroken woman coming out of a failed intimate relationship, would not tell her it was her fault for getting too close to another person, but would partner with her on the path toward healing.

My changing view of God's character meant I had to rethink the role of a Christian—not to live a perfect life, avoiding any scrapes and bruises, but rather to make mistakes in the pursuit of loving others.

The text that shaped this view was The Irresistible Revolution by Shane Claiborne. Claiborne tells a story about Mother Teresa: He noticed her feet were deformed and asked why—and was told that all their possessions were donated, and when shoes were donated, she always took the worst pair. As a result, her feet became deformed.

Until this point I saw my role as a Christian to keep my white shoes clean, and help other people keep their shoes clean, too. In his story, Mother Teresa served God by allowing her feet to become warped permanently. A meaningful and godly life was not about purity, but about service and sacrifice.

United Church of Christ pastor Bromleigh McCleneghan says it best in her book, Good Christian Sex: "The call of the gospel is not to protect ourselves at all costs, but to risk ourselves in love."

What changed for me about sex had little to do with sex itself and everything to do with theology.

The uniquely Christian aspect of this viewpoint on sex is how it interplays with the concept of grace, a central theme of the Bible. The message, which as an evangelical Christian I was taught to spread, is that Jesus died on a cross to redeem us from our sins. Humans were born sinners, and the death of Jesus, who was perfect and never sinned, would symbolically provide forgiveness for all the sins, or wrongdoings, of every other person who lived. "Grace" is sometimes defined as an acronym, God's Riches at Christ's Expense, with Christ meaning Jesus and the riches referring to eternal life.

Grace isn't just about getting to heaven. We love because God first loved us, Christians will say. There's a Bible story in which someone asks Jesus how many times he has to forgive someone who wronged him—seven times? No, seven times seventy times, Jesus answers. The interpretation here is that there should be no limit to forgiveness. God forgives us of all things, and we should forgive others of all things.

The more difficult question for me is why the world was created this way in the first place. Why not just make perfect people with no sin? No sickness? No hate? Why introduce the potential for wrongdoing, then forgive? God didn't create a world where only "perfect" happens, and further, he didn't seem to desire a perfect standard. The Bible is filled with underdog characters who have broken the treasured rules of their societies. The Bible is not a story of the straight and narrow, or of purity. It's a story of people getting their hands dirty.

The Bible condemns the religious people who walked right by the beaten traveler and uplifts the "Samaritan" who risks his own well-being to help. Risking heartbreak and pregnancy, even with protection, to show affection to a fellow human being seems oddly parallel.

The final barrier to fall down was my fantasy of marrying the hot pastor, or otherwise upstanding Christian man, whom God would want me to be with.

Since childhood, I imagined that my future husband would be better than anything I could dream up. He'd be more attractive than the guitar player at church I was afraid to talk to; he'd be strong and tall, read his Bible every day, and impress my parents.

He'd care that I was a virgin; he would be one, too, and it would make all those years of waiting worth it. "I saved myself for you," we would say to each other.

But even as a virgin, I no longer wanted to marry a guy who specifically wanted to marry a virgin. That desire presupposed there was something uniquely sinful about sex that couldn't be forgiven. And such a belief had no place in my new Christianity.

Now, I wanted to lose my virginity not in spite of my faith but because of it.

Between knowledge and observation up to this point, I was tipping toward believing there was absolutely nothing wrong, Christian or otherwise, about sex before marriage. The only piece left was experience. Perhaps if I tried sex, I would understand why it was so important to avoid. After all, a forgiving God would always take me back if I turned out to be wrong.

NEW YORK CITY

My final church crush was a guy who started a nonprofit that spray-painted designs on Bibles and left them places for people to find, as a sort of grassroots evangelism. I read on his blog that he had been sexually active but now, as a Christian, he was dedicated to waiting. I was sad because I was now a Christian who wanted to have sex—at least, try it, and maybe go back to waiting afterwards.

But before anything could happen between us, I got laid off from my job at a journalism startup and moved to New York City.

My parents supported the move, knowing part of the reason was for better career opportunities, but my dad still slipped and told me New York was a present-day Babylon (a "city of sin" described in sections of the Bible thought to be referencing the future).

In New York, nobody knew I was a Christian. Just like with the swim team girls and my former roommates, I wanted to stay quiet about my faith in order to observe the lives of others. Perhaps even more than that, I wanted to observe myself. Who would I become when I wasn't around my Christian friends, who expected me to only date other Christians and never spend the night outside of my own apartment?

I still wasn't prepared for the social norms in the big city.

When I told a coworker about my bedroom setup, with a loft bed to make better use of the small space and tall ceiling, she joked that I could just go to the guy's house for sexual encounters. I was appalled that she thought I'd be so promiscuous as to sleep with not just a boyfriend, but a stranger.

What was most strange, though, was that she

didn't refer to hooking up as a promiscuous thing—in fact, she referenced it on a subway platform, in public, as if it was totally normal. It made me wonder if I could become the person she thought I was: a respectful person, with good morals, who was sexually active—something I had believed to be a contradiction until now.

"Sex positivity" refers to a movement that treats all sexual experiences as good, as long as they are safe and consensual. There's an emphasis on comprehensive sexual education. This is what my friend implied when she referenced a hookup with no judgment—I was an adult, so why shouldn't I have sex for pleasure with whomever I wanted?

My upbringing was the opposite of this. Instead of education, I was given fear. And long after I decided God thought sex was OK, I was limited in how I could act on it, because I didn't know how sex worked or how to initiate it. No wonder ignorance is used to drive abstinence. It works!

Moving to New York forced me to face things I already knew about myself, under the surface: that I wasn't sure when I would get married, if ever—the career thing was going really well—and that avoiding intimacy to guarantee a great marriage was a bad strategy.

My friends who got married as virgins right out of college may have avoided unnecessary heartbreak by not having sex in high school and college relationships, but if I were to get married at 35 without a prior intimate relationship, I would be a decade behind in terms of building relational skills that are relevant to romantic relationships. It seemed like I wasn't doing anyone any favors—definitely not my future husband.

And in a new city where nobody knew of my conservative upbringing, I felt a newfound freedom to act on what I already knew.

I rode the subway, holding onto the center pole, observing strangers, looking for single men. I wondered what would happen if I approached one and blatantly invited him to have sex. Pop culture told me men never say no to sex, but was it true? I pictured myself naked in someone else's sheets, their sweaty skin next to mine.

It was 2012, I was 26, and I'd watched season 1 of Girls twice, seeing Shoshanna get flat-out rejected by an intimate partner after admitting it's her first time.

76

Apparently post-teen virgins were not desirable but a liability. This was a slight improvement from The 40-Year-Old Virgin, where sexual status is a punch line.

Now that I rejected purity as an essential piece of my Christian identity, I was free to have sex. In fact, I was determined to, because I felt that by experiencing it firsthand, I could finally say whether it was right or wrong. But how does one start? Somehow, I needed to find someone I was comfortable with. Maybe another former conservative Christian? Someone unlikely to have those mysterious diseases I still knew little about? But, it needed to be someone I wouldn't date, because I wasn't going to tell him it was my first time.

All those years, I dreamed of "giving" my virginity to a deserving husband. It was a one-time gift that would bond us together for life.

But as a single Christian who was having sex, I needed my virginity to be wholly my own.

I didn't want any average guy to be able to say he took my virginity. The symbolism of virginity in Christian circles—something to preserve so you can wear white on your wedding—was what I wanted to reject. I didn't want it to hold weight. But in a small way, I was also mourning my loss—not the loss of virginity, but giving up on the fantasy that saving my virginity meant God would provide a perfect husband. It was just me and God now, and I was going to find out if he really cared about premarital sex. Loss of virginity wasn't a moment I was going to share with some guy. The memory, and its significance, needed to be mine.

I just needed to address an impossible situation, which is: How does a nice Christian girl who has barely dated navigate from acquaintances . . . to sex?

As with all things in life that were outside of my control, I resorted to prayer. God answered with an underground bar that serves drinks in pineapples.

SAN FRANCISCO

It was my second time at a technology conference, and this year it was held in San Francisco. The weather was warm; the ocean seemed to be everywhere you looked, and it smelled delightful. I was still new to living in New York, and coming back to my native California gave me second thoughts, making me wonder if I had chosen the wrong city. The first night of the conference kicked off with margaritas at a local Mexican restaurant and bar. I quickly caught up with acquaintances I had met the year before, and then we walked over to the second event together—a dinner.

"I'm in New York now," I'd start each time I ran into an old contact, quickly filling in friends on the demise of the startup I was working for the year prior, and moving on to my new role at a well-known media company, which held more gravitas in this circle. The networking was going well, and I just needed a quick pit stop before I kept going.

When I came out of the restroom, my group was gone. I figured I'd get in the food line and find them later.

I am one of those people who believes in something like fate, and when anything significant happens, I sort through every choice leading up to it, wondering if, had I turned right instead of left, or worn the other dress, I would be out of luck completely. Something like fate was at play on this night.

So I don't know how I got there, if it was the fact I was wearing my favorite grey V-neck, or if my bladder was simply in sync with my heart, but there I was in the food line when I realized the guy behind me had come to the conference the year before, too. We'd had a great conversation, he was really smart and thoughtful, and we'd followed each other on Twitter. He'd once posted a story about a stranger showing him photos of her dog at a park when she accidentally swiped to a self-nude, a story that still makes me laugh when I think about it.

I hadn't thought of him much in the past year, since he lived in a different city. But here he was, again. He started telling me about growing up riding horses, how he hacked a local politician's website when he was 14, and his obsession with the AMC show Mad Men. Soon we were eating together, which turned into going out for drinks with his coworkers.

Matthew was a software engineer and well respected by the much older men who reported to him at his company, but at first glance, he could easily be mistaken for the marketing intern—he had messy, curly brown hair and the perfect amount of stubble. He was an attentive listener, and unlike most highly driven guys I knew, he seemed to take my ideas and aspirations as seriously as his own.

When the night wound down, Matthew suggested we go back to the hotel bar together for one more drink, just the two of us. When the hotel bar turned out to be closed, we went up to his room. We started kissing. We lay down on his bed. Then he pulled down my V-neck T-shirt and stretched it to each side to kiss my breasts.

"I didn't prepare for this, but I could run down to the corner store," he said. "Be back in 10 minutes?"

It took me a moment to translate what he was saying, and I realized he was implying he wanted to have sex (exciting!), that we should use a condom (good thing), but he didn't have one (bad thing).

This all happened rather fast—apparently the acquaintances-to-sex formula is easier than I expected—but it's fair to say I didn't know how quickly these things normally happen. Before this, I hadn't had a boyfriend and could probably count the times I had kissed someone on one hand.

"It's OK, maybe another time," I said, wanting both the safety of a condom and the extra time to be sure I was making the right choice. He offered to walk me back to my hotel—it was late, and it was a mile back to my budget Chinatown hotel room where I could sleep on a twin bed with a rock-hard mattress. But I refused, determined to be self-sufficient in my walk back in the dark.

"Can I see you tomorrow night?" he asked, making his intentions clear. I happily agreed.

It was late the next afternoon that I got his text. "I got a recommendation for a good place," he wrote. "They serve drinks in pineapples!"

We planned to meet up later, but as conferences go, there were several open-bar sponsored parties running through the evening. That's how I found myself drunk on free beer inside a Google office, with minutes to spare and a 10-minute drive or 30-minute walk ahead of me. San Francisco is not known for its cabs, so I set off on a fast walk. Unfortunately, it slipped my mind that San Francisco is known for its hills. I know the love songs go on about running one thousand miles for love, but I had never truly felt it until this night, when I would have scaled Mount Everest to meet Matthew.

Between dashing across streets and pulling out my phone to make sure I was walking the right way, I dropped my iPhone a few blocks from the bar, getting the first-ever crack in its screen. For three years I had preserved that phone, crack-free. The coincidence of my phone's loss of purity and impending loss of purity of my body was not lost on me.

I was half an hour late and was apologetic about it. He'd already ordered our drinks, so I gulped down the pineapple drink, despite already being drunk from the earlier party. After the tiki bar, we went to North Beach, where we danced and then kissed, until the bar's security guy tapped us on the shoulder to indicate we should stop. (Public displays of affection are fun!) Then we headed back to his room.

It was dark, and he didn't turn on the light. Unlike the night before, when we'd moved slow, kissing and messing around with our clothes on, this time he got right to business.

He pulled my dress off over my head, and looked at me with eyes wide, like an eight-year-old staring at an ice cream sundae. In preparing for this trip, I hadn't really shaved the private parts of my body, as I would have expected to do before getting naked with someone. But in front of him I felt beautiful, glorious, in my natural, usual, everyday form.

When people talk about sex or even kissing, they say you'll know what to do when you get there. This was somewhat true—I was sufficiently buzzed from drinking, so I didn't have the usual internal monologue questioning my every action. But I was also lucky that he was experienced and took a lot of initiative. For this first-time experience, Matthew was perfect.

I didn't want to admit my virginity. If things went wrong—the sex was bad or I did something embarrassing—I wanted to be able to cut off all contact with the person, and he lived far enough away that I wouldn't need to ever talk to him again, if I didn't want to. But most importantly, I felt comfortable with him. I had met his coworkers, and he wasn't a stranger or brand-new to me. Having met him a year prior gave me a sense of familiarity and safety.

He was on top, then he put me on top. He lifted one leg up over my head, then he was behind me. Then both my legs were straight up in the air, and I was on my back. I rolled around like a doll, and every new position was a brand-new experience. I moved my hips, and we'd sync up in rhythm and then lose it, then find it again.

I didn't have an orgasm.

I assumed I would have an orgasm with Matthew from just having penis-in-vagina sex. Besides, I had been able to orgasm when masturbating.

I would learn later that the ability to reach orgasm during intercourse depends on how close the clitoris is to the vagina[6].

Even without an orgasm, sex was fun. It was really, really fun.

During my years of abstinence, I expected that on my wedding night, I'd finally understand why it was so important to wait. Married Christians seemed to believe so. At the same time, I wondered why non-Christians who were having sex could have missed this, if it were true.

After sex, I now see both. With Matthew, I felt like a goddess. We were naked together and unashamed. It was holy. But it was also tangible and physical and earthly. Just, sex. I felt like we were two

---

6 The optimal distance from clitoris to vagina for orgasms is 2.5 centimeters. If it's further away, as it is for many women, you need to stimulate the clitoris manually.

In a study of singles with familiar partners, 63 percent of women reported having regular orgasms, compared to 85 percent of men (Garcia 2014). There are also anywhere from two to twelve "types" of female orgasms, depending on who you ask, including the most common, the clitoral orgasm; the G-spot orgasm (which is from penetration); and orgasms from nipple stimulation, fantasies, classical music, and even exercise, especially lower-abdominal crunches.

kids, playing in a sandbox, building majestic empires with shovels and buckets.

At this point, I was on my back, legs spread wide. He paused, and ripped open a condom. It had been so important to him the day before to have a condom, so why had he waited until halfway through to use it? I realized thus far we had been having unprotected sex, which made me uncomfortable, but because I was new to this, I was afraid to say something and reveal my naivete.[7]

---

7 At first, I thought perhaps he was only concerned about pregnancy. Semen, which contains sperm, is released during ejaculation, which happens during the male orgasm. It is possible to become pregnant, or get diseases from "pre-ejaculation," so Matthew's method was mostly safe, but not totally safe. Condoms can break or tear, so no protection is perfectly safe.

Some diseases, including HPV, are spread skin-to-skin, so a condom won't completely protect against those. Female birth control—such as pills or an IUD—only protects against pregnancy, and not disease.

It is reasonable to ask a partner to wear a condom throughout intercourse, and had I been paying more attention, I likely would have asked Matthew to do this. Later, if the relationship becomes exclusive, a couple may choose to each get tested for disease and share results, and continue with pregnancy-only protection. This lowers the risk of disease. Also, today sexually transmitted diseases may not all be curable, but they are

After we had intercourse, Matthew lay on his back, looking nearly asleep. I leaned on top of him and kept kissing him, my long hair falling over his forehead. We were having so much fun, and I didn't want to stop.

"You're turning me on again," he said.

"Sorry," I said.

"Sorry" was a weird thing to say. I knew it in the moment, but it took months for me to figure out why. As a conservative Christian, I was taught that wearing short shorts or a two-piece swimsuit could "cause the boys to sin." Now, despite having decided that premarital sex was not a sin, despite being with someone who not only had initiated sex but also was not a Christian, I still had a deep-seated fear that I was "bad" or "wrong" for provoking his desire.

---

far from lethal and can be controlled with medication.

8 This is due to biological limitations that prevent many men from holding an erection after orgasm, but it is also a sexist societal norm.

The hormone prolactin is associated with the amount of time men have to wait between orgasms—which could be anywhere from a few minutes to a full day. However, arousal can enable a man to cut down on this "refractory period," or recovery time.

There was something else about how he said, "You're turning me on ... again"—as if it wasn't entirely positive. One cultural norm of which I was completely unaware was that intercourse is considered over after the male orgasm.[8]

As it turns out, I had nothing to worry about. We did it again.

The next morning, we gathered up our clothing that had been thrown about the room (just like they do in the movies!), and I got ready to head back to my hotel to change clothes before the conference. I paused, looking at his sheets, and noticed a tiny stain of light pink moisture.

"Was that you?" he said, as I paused by the bed.

"I guess so," I replied, seeing something that looked no different than a bit of discharge the last day of your period. My secret was safe, and my virginity was my own.

"That's what housekeeping is for," he said.

It was a beautiful, sunny day in October, the best time of the year in San Francisco. Despite getting little sleep that night, I went back to my hotel and put on my running clothes, and headed out to the Embarcadero that runs along San Francisco's eastern shoreline, dodging tourists and other runners in between glimpses out at the bay lined with boats.

The heavy guilt I expected to feel was nowhere to be found. Even at this point, I was willing to be wrong. I would have happily reverted back and recommitted to abstinence until marriage, or even lifelong celibacy, if I thought that's what God wanted.

But on that run, and the months following, I felt nothing but joy. It turns out this might have been, at least partially, a result of the sex itself.

After sex, my body was changed. My breasts felt larger, and I felt happier and more secure in my body.[9] As time went on, I noticed the discharge on my

---

9 When a woman becomes sexually active, her breasts grow up to 25 percent larger and more firm during the sexual encounter, although they drop back to normal size later. Her nipples become more sensitive, as does her clitoris—these are the woman's centers of pleasure.

During the female orgasm, the vagina expands and contracts, something it doesn't know to do before sex. The vagina becomes more elastic, or more able to expand and contract. Not elastic like a rubber band, but like a muscle that grows stronger with use. This explains why a tampon can be painful to insert, but a penis or a dildo, which terrifyingly looks 10 times larger, can slide in easily when a woman is aroused.

What's really interesting is sex drive. Having sex associates pleasure with the act, thanks to the brain chemical dopamine, and this makes a person want sex more,

underwear when I was aroused was a lot heavier than it had ever been before sex.

One thing I was most anxious about in losing my virginity was that I'd be locked in—that having done it once, I'd want it more, now that I knew what I was missing, and even if I wanted to go back to abstinence until marriage, I wouldn't be able to.

This is silly. I was already aware of my sex drive, despite not knowing what sex was like. As it turns out, though, it's somewhat true: sexual action does increase sex drive.[10] But it's not a permanent effect. After no sex for several months, I was back to normal. Birth control pills also reduce sex drive. As a virgin, I used to masturbate around once per month, and when I had a boyfriend and was on the pill, I had

increasing their sex drive. It's not just the brain, though. After having sex, a woman's clitoris learns to swell up when she is aroused, and her vagina begins lubricating to a greater level.

10 The biological impact of having sex is perhaps more significant than losing one's virginity. Sex boosts neurogenesis, or the creation of new brain neurons, which improves cognitive function (Glasper 2013). Regular sex boosts the immune system (Charnetski 2004), and heterosexual intercourse is associated with better mental and physical performance, as well as lower stress levels (Brody, 2005), which would explain the lasting happiness following my weekend of sexual intimacy.

almost no sex drive at all, despite having regular sex.

NO SHAME

When I got back to New York after the conference, I felt like a new woman. As I listened to love songs on my subway commute to work, they no longer were distant or aspirational. I had been the object of someone's affection, and I had felt these feelings.

Matthew was a "first" in more ways than one. I'd had crushes throughout my life, even some that seemed mutual, at least if you're counting the times you catch a guy staring at you from across the room, as my shy, younger self did. I'd gone on a few dates. But the type of guys I idolized and obsessed over were never the same ones who were interested in me. While other guys had invited me to breakfast after a yoga class, or to browse free museums on a Saturday, Matthew had asked me to drinks and then paid the bill, in a way that made it clear that it was a date, and that I was desired. More importantly, I desired him. It was mutual.

The affirmation that I was desired and was desirable stayed with me for months. Even after Matthew and I quit texting, and I cried, realizing that in two different cities there was no romantic future for us, I still had the memory and the knowledge that romantic love was available to me.

For so many years I believed that marriage was a difficult but rewarding endeavor, but sex could help facilitate its longevity, a sort of icing on top. One of my most surprising discoveries after having sex is that sex itself takes patience and effort. And abstaining from sex doesn't circumvent relationship baggage, but brings baggage of its own.

My difficulties in reaching an orgasm during intercourse were not resolved in one night. They continued through my first committed relationship. Despite deciding I was willing to be in an intimate but nonmarried relationship, I still retained a level of distrust of my boyfriend, subconsciously believing that because he was willing to sleep with me before marriage, he didn't really love me.

At the same time, I withdrew from my Christian family and friends, scared they would reject me if they found out my boyfriend and I went on overnight trips together, which would imply I was no longer a virgin. In fact, I lied about it. My earlier judgments of people who had sex followed me, and now I worried I would be judged and rejected by those closest to me.

I felt so strongly about this that I once considered returning to abstinence—not because I thought God cared, but because I wanted to preserve the safety net of my family and closest friends.

The greatest doubt I experience over my decision to not save sex for marriage comes up each time I attend the wedding of a Christian friend. I used to think non-Christian weddings were boring—the couple might already live together, and they've obviously had sex, so all the wedding represents is a party, whereas at a Christian wedding, everyone knows the couple is going to have sex for the very first time that same night, and the two will become one.

"I am glad I was faithful to you throughout our courtship so I know I can be faithful in marriage," a friend's husband said in his vows. The translation out of Christianese is this: He didn't have sex with her, and if he had, neither of them could trust him to not have sex with other people after they were married. This was the same message I heard all those years ago from the celebrity pastor, and it's one that's still hard to shake.

It wasn't until my relationship with my first boyfriend was over that I realized why I constantly worried he would cheat on me when none of his actions gave me any reason to believe that. That nagging message was still stuck in the back of my brain—he wanted to have sex with me without being married, and therefore he didn't love me and would surely cheat on me.

When my Christian friends get married, I also wonder why it's not me. I wonder if, had I waited just a year or two longer, God would have provided the hot pastor after all, and now I will live out the rest of my years alone because I broke the sex rule. I wonder if it's not too late.

Of course, my non-Christian roommates, the ones who started their relationship with casual sex, are married now, too. Many of the girls I went to high school with—who I judged for having sex back when I didn't know about the clitoris and thought sex was obscene—are now married with kids of their own in the suburbs.

Meanwhile, I'm also back in the city where I lost my virginity—San Francisco, one of the most liberal cities in the country, where sex positivity is the norm. That doesn't mean I'm having sex all the time. I'm still finding out what I like.

I work across the street from the Embarcadero where I went for that joyful run, and I've been back to the bar where Matthew and I had drinks in pineapples. It's comforting to be here, and to remember that I took a risk, and God stayed with me.

Afterword

We are at a powerful moment in history. Sixty-one percent of Christians now say they would have sex before marriage (ChristianMingle & JDate 2014). Another study found that 80 percent of unmarried evangelical young adults said they have had sex, not too much lower than 88 percent of all unmarried adults (National Campaign to Prevent Teen and Unplanned Pregnancy 2009). My story is just one of many.

When I set out to write this book, I imagined that without abstinence until marriage as a standard, I would define a new set of values to guide my decisions around intimate relationships—new morals that could be an example for others to follow. Perhaps I'd always wait until the third date and avoid anal sex, or something like that. The problem is, I recognize that I still yearn for these rules as a way to protect myself.

But intimacy is about trusting and faith.

The lesson of my rethinking around purity is not that virginity is the wrong standard, one to be replaced by a new moral guideline. The lesson is that God's love is infinite. It's that I can't look to rules to help me live up to God's standard. It's that, when my heart gets broken, maybe by someone I slept with, that God is there to comfort, not judge me.

The most sexually charged section of the Bible, Song of Solomon, is explained by some to be an allegory of God's relationship with people. There is no shortage of analogies between God's love and human relationships, even sexual relationships between unmarried people. I've learned in greater depth the meaning of unconditional love and how God loves me through my intimate relationships, even though I am not married.

I once read that you'll feel guilty on your wedding day if you've slept with other people. That you'll look in your fiancé's eyes and know that you can never be 100 percent with him because you've given pieces of yourself to others.

Perhaps sex is less like giving something away and more like exchanging. Bodily fluids, sure, but it's also like a chemical reaction, and after you both go your separate ways, you are each forever changed. Not every intimate encounter or relationship ends well. But even the worst ones, for me, have built resilience, have taught me about my deep-seated needs, and have helped me become a better partner. My exes propelled me towards the happiness I find now or will find in the future, and for that, I am grateful. This is redemption.

I've learned sex before marriage does have consequences. As C. S. Lewis wrote in The Four Loves:

"To love at all is to be vulnerable. Love anything and your heart will be wrung and possibly broken. If you want to make sure of keeping it intact you must give it to no one, not even an animal. Wrap it carefully round with hobbies and little luxuries; avoid all entanglements. Lock it up safe in the casket or coffin of your selfishness. But in that casket, safe, dark, motionless, airless, it will change. It

will not be broken; it will become
unbreakable, impenetrable, irredeemable. To
love is to be vulnerable."

When I set out to avoid sex, I was actually
resisting love. Sex is a physical act that consummates
whatever range of feelings are present, with results
both magical and tragic.

Now I know that any shame associated with
intimacy does not come from God. The loving God of
the Bible is there to pick up the pieces, to extinguish the
shame and move forward. I'm able to love more
deeply, not in spite of the pain but because of it. When
I'm able to love, I am able to know God, because God is
love, after all.

Your Turn

Share your thoughts on sex and single Christians with #ShamelessTheBook

or email hi@danifankhauser.com to tell me your story.

Find more of my writing at shamelessthebook.com.

Bibliography

Brody S1. "Blood pressure reactivity to stress is better for people who recently had penile-vaginal intercourse than for people who had other or no sexual activity." Biological Psychology. 2006 Feb;71(2):214-22. Epub 2005 Jun 14.

Charnetski CJ, Brennan FX. "Sexual frequency and salivary immunoglobulin A (IgA)." Psychological Reports [01 Jun 2004, 94(3 Pt 1):839-844]. DOI: 10.2466/PR0.94.3.839-844.

ChristianMingle & JDate. Second Annual State of Dating in America. Los Angeles: Spark.net, 2014. Accessed September 14, 2017.

http://www.spark.net/christianmingle-and-jdate-release-second-annual-state-of-dating-in-america-report/

Deutschländer, S., Güntürkün, O., Hurlemann, R., Kendrick, K.M., Maier, W., Scheele, D., Striepens, N. "Oxytocin Modulates Social Distance between Males and Females." Journal of Neuroscience 14 November 2012, 32 (46) 16074-16079; DOI: https://doi.org/10.1523/JNEUROSCI.2755-12.2012.

Garcia, J. R., Lloyd, E. A., Wallen, K. and Fisher, H. E. "Variation in Orgasm Occurrence by Sexual Orientation in a Sample of U.S. Singles." Journal of Sexual Medicine 11, 11 (2014). 2645–2652. doi:10.1111/jsm.12669.

Glasper ER1, Gould E. "Sexual experience restores age-related decline in adult neurogenesis and hippocampal function." Hippocampus. 2013 Apr;23(4):303-12. doi: 10.1002/hipo.22090. Epub 2013 Mar 5.

Macdonald K1, Macdonald TM. "The peptide

that binds: a systematic review of oxytocin and its prosocial effects in humans." Harvard Review of Psychiatry 2010 Jan-Feb;18(1):1-21. doi: 10.3109/10673220903523615.

National Campaign to Prevent Teen and Unplanned Pregnancy. Magical Thinking: Young Adults' Attitudes and Beliefs About Sex, Contraception, and Unplanned Pregnancy. Washington DC: National Campaign to Prevent Teen and Unplanned Pregnancy, 2009. Accessed September 14, 2017. https://thenationalcampaign.org/resource/magical-thinking

Acknowledgments

Thanks to Bianca, Addie, Jasmeet, Erin, Isabella, Mariya, Evan, and Earnest for reading early drafts of this book, my editors, Vonnie York and Jennifer Rubio, my allies in Dreamers//Doers and Binders, and to Demi Lovato, Jess Glynne, Kesha, and Reese Witherspoon for making art that celebrates powerful women.

Made in the USA
Coppell, TX
13 February 2021